Let's Play Tag!

 Read the Page

▶ Read the Story

🔄 Repeat

⬛ Stop

⭐ Game

🙂 Yes

☹ No

TO USE THIS BOOK WITH THE TAG™ READER you must download audio from the LeapFrog Connect application. The LeapFrog Connect application can be installed from the CD provided with your Tag Reader or at leapfrog.com/tag.

For my Dad —D.C.
To Sue Dooley —B.L.

CLICK, CLACK, MOO
Cows That Type

by Doreen Cronin pictures by Betsy Lewin

Farmer Brown has a problem.
His cows like to type.
All day long he hears

Click, clack, **moo.**
Click, clack, **moo.**
Clickety, clack, **moo.**

 At first, he couldn't believe his ears.
Cows that type?
Impossible!

Click, clack, **moo.**
　Click, clack, **moo.**
Clickety, clack, **moo.**

Then, he couldn't believe his eyes.

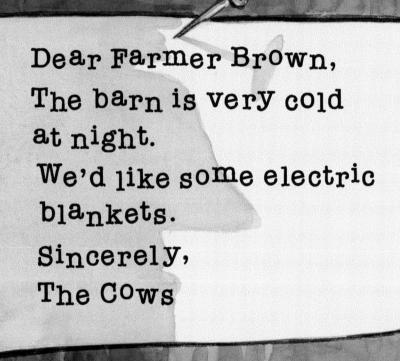

Dear Farmer Brown,
The barn is very cold
at night.
We'd like some electric
blankets.
Sincerely,
The Cows

It was bad enough the cows had found the old typewriter in the barn, now they wanted electric blankets! "No way," said Farmer Brown. "No electric blankets."

So the cows went on strike. They left a note on the barn door.

8

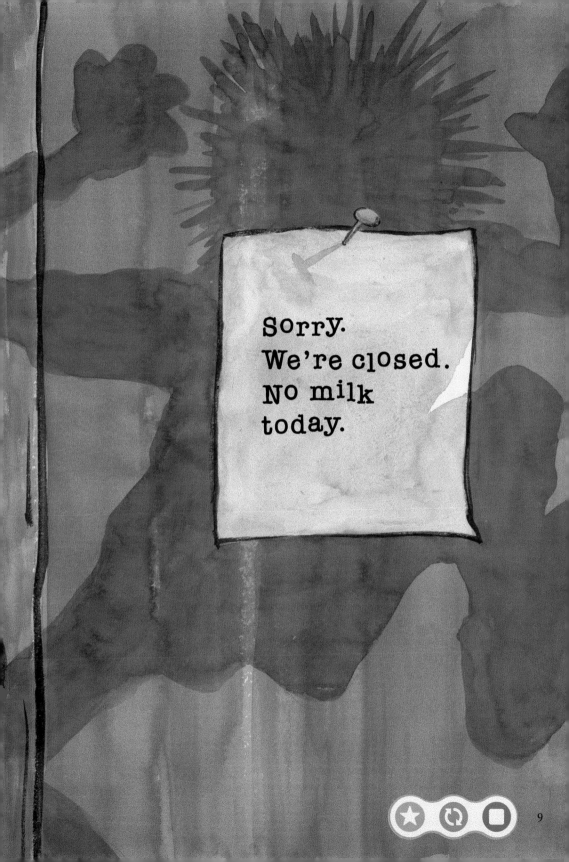

 "No milk today!" cried Farmer
Brown. In the background, he
heard the cows busy at work:

Click, clack, **moo.**
Click, clack, **moo.**
Clickety, clack, **moo.**

The next day, he got
another note:

Dear Farmer Brown,
The hens are cold too.
They'd like electric
blankets.
Sincerely,
The Cows

The cows were growing impatient with the farmer. They left a new note on the barn door.

"No eggs!" cried Farmer Brown.
In the background he heard
them.

Click, clack, **moo.**
 Click, clack, **moo.**
 Clickety, clack, **moo.**

"Cows that type. Hens on strike! Whoever heard of such a thing? How can I run a farm with no milk and no eggs!" Farmer Brown was furious.

Farmer Brown got out his own typewriter.

Dear Cows and Hens:

There will be no electric blankets.
You are cows and hens.
I demand milk and eggs.

Sincerely,
Farmer Brown

 Duck was a neutral party, so he brought the ultimatum to the cows.

The cows held an emergency meeting. All the animals gathered around the barn to snoop, but none of them could understand Moo.

All night long, Farmer Brown waited for an answer.

Duck knocked on the door early the next morning. He handed Farmer Brown a note:

Dear Farmer Brown,
We will exchange our typewriter
for electric blankets.
Leave them outside the barn door
and we will send Duck over
with the typewriter.

Sincerely,
The Cows

25

Farmer Brown decided this was a good deal. He left the blankets

next to the barn door and waited for
Duck to come with the typewriter.

The next morning
he got a note:

> Dear Farmer Brown,
> The pond is quite boring.
> We'd like a diving board.
> Sincerely,
> The Ducks

Click, clack, **quack.**
Click, clack, **quack.**
Clickety, clack, **quack.**